Kitty
You are now entering a Gaskitts book
yawn

First published 2001 by Walker Books Ltd
87 Vauxhall Walk, London SE11 5HJ

This edition published 2012

2 4 6 8 10 9 7 5 3

This book has been typeset in Stempel Schneidler,
Cafeteria, Tapioca and Kosmik

Printed in Thailand

British Library Cataloguing in Publication Data:
a catalogue record for this book
is available from the British Library

ISBN 978-1-4063-4155-3

www.walker.co.uk

Allan Ahlberg

The Man Who Wore All His Clothes

illustrated by
KATHARINE McEWEN

WALKER BOOKS
AND SUBSIDIARIES
LONDON • BOSTON • SYDNEY • AUCKLAND

Contents

Meet The Gaskitts

Mr Gaskitt

A slim young father who sometimes wears all his clothes.

Mrs Gaskitt

A loving mother and hard-working taxi-driver.

Gus and Gloria Gaskitt

Nine-year-old twins.

Horace:
the Gaskitts' Cat

Likes easy chairs,
old movies on TV
and cat food ads.

The Gaskitts' Refrigerator

Five-star freezer,
large vegetable
compartment,
good speller.

The Gaskitts'
Car Radio

Sometimes gets
things wrong.

Chapter One
Mr Gaskitt Gets Dressed

One morning in the month of December

Mr Gaskitt got up.

He put on his vest and pants and socks,

and his socks and vest and pants,

and his pants and socks and vest.

"Lovely socks, dear," said Mrs Gaskitt.

He put on his three shirts and
his two pairs of trousers.
"Very smart, Dad," said Gloria.

He put on four jumpers and a t
"Great tie, Dad," Gus said.

Meanwhile, Horace had jumped into Mr Gaskitt's still-warm bed.

All of a sudden, the phone rang.

"I want a taxi," said a gruff voice.

"Right," said Mrs Gaskitt. "When for?"

"In half an hour – on the dot."

"Right," said Mrs Gaskitt.

"Where from?"

"Pick me up outside the bank," said the voice.

"Right," said Mrs Gaskitt. "And where will I take you to?"

"As far away as possible," said the voice.

"Only joking lady!" and he hung up.

Mr Gaskitt ate his breakfast.

He put on his jacket,

his anorak,

his overcoat,

his three scarves,

his two pairs of gloves

and his plastic mac.

“Don’t forget

your hats, dear,”

said Mrs Gaskitt.

Mr Gaskitt kissed his wife and children –

"Goodbye, darlings!"

"Bye-bye, Dad!"

– and left the house.

Chapter Two
Mr Gaskitt Gets Stuck

Mr Gaskitt squeezed into his car.

A little snow had begun to fall.

He switched on the radio.

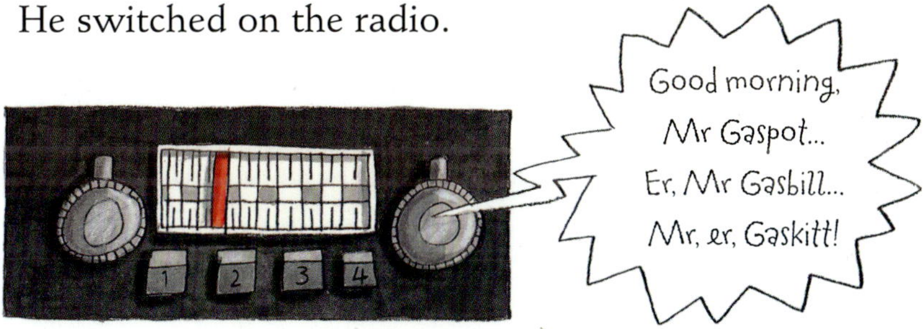

"I must get that radio fixed,"

thought Mr Gaskitt.

He drove down the road,

round the roundabout

and up and over the flyover.

He stopped at the traffic lights:

red – amber – green.

Meanwhile, Horace had come downstairs and was watching TV in the sitting-room.

Mrs Gaskitt was parked outside the bank.

Gus and Gloria were at school watching – Oh no! – their poor old teacher falling down from a ladder.

The teacher's name was Mrs Fritter. She landed with a dreadful bang, got a big lump on her head and had to go home.

Back in the car, Mr Gaskitt was stuck in the traffic.

A lorry had tipped over while trying to reverse.

"STAND CLEAR!

I AM REVERSING!

BEEP, BEEP!

I AM STILL REVERSING!

BEEP!

I AM SKIDDING!

I AM FALLING OVER!

BEEEEP!"

Now the lorry's load of Christmas trees

was rolling around all over the street.

The lorry itself was lying on its side.

Mr Gaskitt sighed and
twiddled with his radio.
"The roads are clear,"
the radio said.
"No hold-ups anywhere.
A happy Easter to all
our listeners."

Chapter Three

Mr Gaskitt Gets Going Again

The road was clear and the sun was shining.

Mr Gaskitt was on his way again.

"Terrible traffic jams," said the radio.

"Fog everywhere!

Eat Mrs Mossop's mince pies."

Mr Gaskitt stopped at the petrol station.

He got: 4 free wine glasses

3 car stickers

2 cans of Slugg

1 packet of Protts

a giant economy bag of popcorn –

oh yes, and some petrol.

Meanwhile, Horace had left the house and was visiting a friend.

Gus and Gloria were getting into trouble with the supply teacher, whose name was Mr Blotter.

The problem was,

Mr Blotter had not taught for many years.

His ways were somewhat …

… old-fashioned.

BANK

Meanwhile also, outside the bank

Mrs Gaskitt was getting impatient.

Just as she was about to leave – Bang! –

out of the bank rushed a small man.

He had his collar turned up and

his hat turned down.

He was carrying an enormous bag.

"Where to?" said Mrs Gaskitt.

"Er, the airport," growled the man.

"Shall I put your bag in the boot?"

"Er, no."

The man clutched his bag and

looked over his shoulder.

"I'd rather hold on to it."

Chapter Four
Mrs Gaskitt Smells a Rat

Mr Gaskitt was driving along.

"Soon be there now," he said to himself.

The radio was playing a rock 'n' roll song.

Suddenly a voice said,

"We interrupt this rock 'n' roll song

with a newsflash:

THERE HAS BEEN A ROBBERY AT THE BANK!"

"Fancy that," said Mr Gaskitt.

"THE POLICE ARE ON THE LOOKOUT

FOR A BAD MAN WITH A SMALL BOG,"

said the radio.

"NO, ER, A LARGE
MAN WITH A BAD
BACK. A
SMALL BAG
WITH A ...
OH, DEAR."

Mrs Gaskitt had her radio on too.

"Wow, a robbery at the bank!" she cried.

"Dreadful," growled her passenger, and he clutched his bag closer.

"You got out of that bank just in time," said Mrs Gaskitt.

"Yeah," growled the man. "Lucky, wasn't it?"

Just then a police siren began to sound in the street behind them.

"Step on it," growled the man.

But Mrs Gaskitt was getting suspicious.

"Why should I?"

"Because I say so," growled the man.

Mrs Gaskitt smelled a rat.

"Wait a minute – what have you got in that bag?"

"Mind your own business,"

growled the man.

And he said,

"Turn left."

Meanwhile, Gus and Gloria were having more trouble with Mr Blotter.

"Fingers on lips!"

"Elbows on knees!"

"Left legs behind necks and over right shoulders!" said Mr Blotter.

Meanwhile also, Horace was at his friend's house watching an old movie.

It was a sad old movie.

Horace had his hankie out.

Suddenly a voice said,

"We interrupt this sad old movie with a newsflash:

THERE HAS BEEN A ROBBERY AT THE BANK!"

Back at the school, the children

were setting off for the swimming-baths.

Mr Blotter was marching them

like soldiers on parade across the playground.

Meanwhile, out in the street

the bus was waiting.

School Bus

Chapter Five

Run Robber Run

Mr Gaskitt was still driving along and

his radio was still getting things wrong.

"THE ROBBER IS MAKING HIS GETAWAY

ON A MOTORBIKE," said the radio.

Meanwhile, the robber

was still in Mrs Gaskitt's taxi.

"THE ROBBER IS MAKING HIS

GETAWAY ON A FIRE ENGINE!"

yelled the radio.

Meanwhile, Mrs Gaskitt

had stopped at the traffic lights

and the robber had jumped out.

"THE ROBBER IS HIDING AWAY IN HIS SECRET DEN EATING EGG, CHIPS AND BEANS!" hollered the radio.

Meanwhile, the robber

was wondering what to do next.

Just then he spotted the bus.

It was waiting at the traffic lights too.

Small round faces were pressed

against the steamy glass.

One or two of them had their tongues out.

Meanwhile, Mrs Gaskitt wa

chasing the robber.

"Stop thief!" she cried.

Down the street, the police

siren was getting louder.

The robber opened

the door of the bus and jumped in.

Gus and Gloria were sitting on the front seat

with their swimming bags.

Mr Blotter stood up in the gangway.

"Who are you?" he said.

"Mind your own business," growled the man.

And to the driver he said, "Step on it!"

Chapter Six

"Miaow!" said Horace

Mr Gaskitt was

still driving

along.

Up ahead he thought he could see

Mrs Gaskitt's taxi.

Mrs Gaskitt was

running after the bus.

She thought *she* could see

Gus and Gloria.

Meanwhile, inside the bus Mr Blotter was asking, "What's all this? What's going on?"

And the children were telling him.

"It's a hijack, Sir!"

"A kidnappin'!"

"Ransom!"

"No, it ain't – it's a joke!"

"A trick!"

"He's pullin' our legs!"

Now the robber took charge.

From his pocket he pulled … a gun.

Well, a toy gun, actually,

the one he'd used in the bank.

"That ain't real!" yelled the children.

"I've got one of them!"

"It's plastic!"

"Silence!" growled the robber. "Blasted kids."

And he said, "Fingers on lips – hands on heads."

He was old-fashioned too.

Then to Mr Blotter he said, "And you!"

And to the driver, "Drive!"

DRIVE!
School Bus
SKOOL 4 YOU

The chase began.

The bus drove down the street.

Mrs Gaskitt in her taxi chased after it.

Mr Gaskitt in his car chased after her.

And the police chased after him.

And the *TV news reporter,*

with her TV camera man and her TV van,

chased after them.

TV2000

Meanwhile, Horace was at his friend's house

watching TV.

It was a cat food ad for Crunchy Mice,

Horace's favourite food.

Suddenly, a voice said,

"We interrupt this cat food ad

for Crunchy Mice with live coverage of …

A POLICE CHASE!"

"Miaow!" said Horace.

Chapter Seven

The Unhappy Robber

The bus went up the hill

and down the hill.

The children began

to whisper.

Into the underpass and out of it.

The children began to talk.

Round the roundabout

and up and over the flyover.

The children began to yell.

"Whee!"

"Please, Sir," (to the robber),

"I feel sick!"

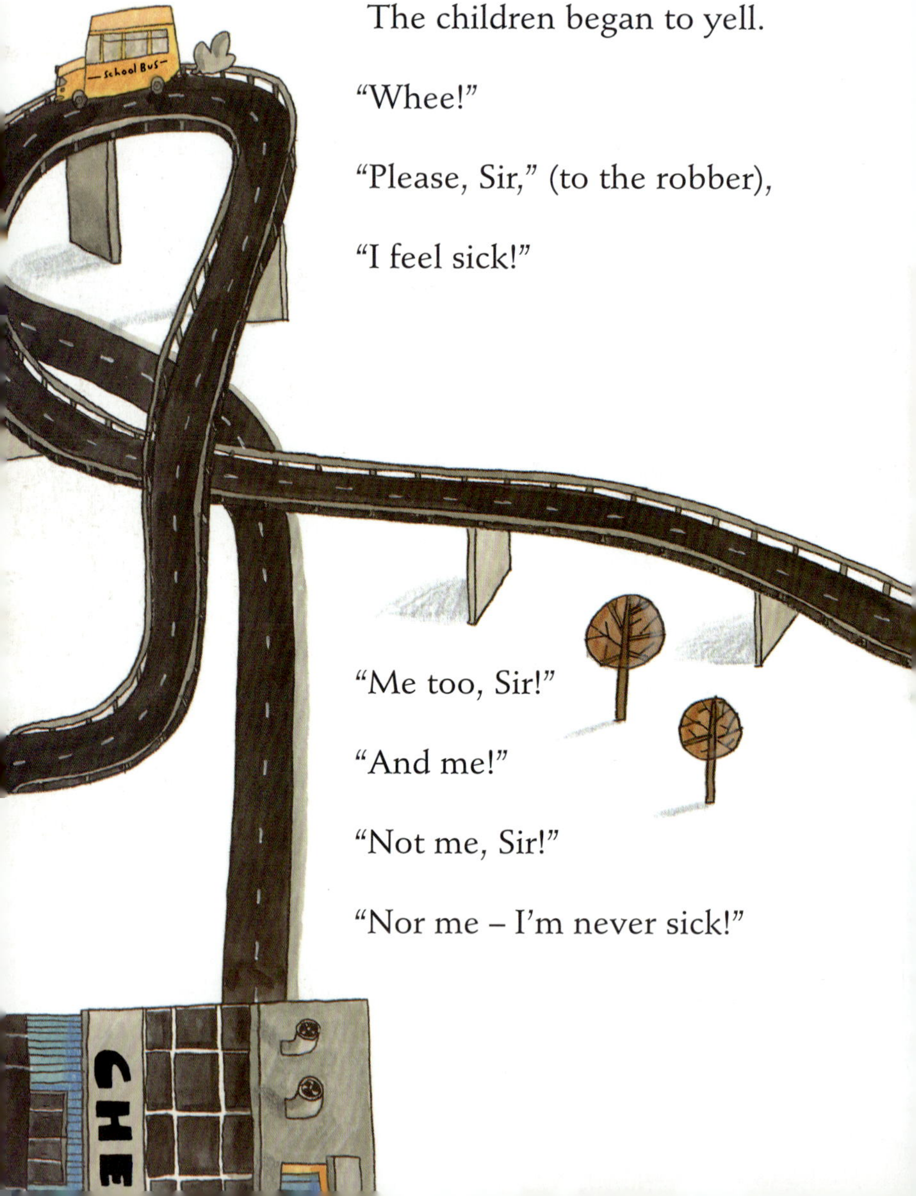

"Me too, Sir!"

"And me!"

"Not me, Sir!"

"Nor me – I'm never sick!"

"Silence!" growled the robber, but the children were now so noisy they couldn't hear him.

"Please, Sir, Tracey's got my swimming goggles!"

"Jonathan's got my towel!"

"Brian's eating, Sir!"

"Are we nearly there now?"

The robber felt trapped.

He put his hands over his ears.

"This is worse than being in jail," he thought.

Meanwhile, Mr Blotter was smiling.

"Please, Sir!"

The noise grew louder still.

"*Please*, Sir!"

"He's got my—"

"Mr Robber!"

"No, I never!"

"Yes, you did!"

"That's not fair!"

"Mr *Robber!*"

"Stop pushin'!"

Meanwhile, "Mr Robber" was unhappy.

He looked out into the crowded, *peaceful* street.

And, "Stop the bus!" he cried.

Chapter Eight

Mr Gaskitt Lends a Hand

Mr Gaskitt was *racing* along.

He was a worried man.

What was Mrs Gaskitt up to?

Why was she chasing that bus?

Mrs Gaskitt was also racing.

She was a worried woman.

What was that robber up to?

Where was he going with

Gus and Gloria?

Suddenly the bus stopped.

Out jumped the robber

closely followed by Mr Blotter,

the driver and twenty-seven children …

all yelling.

"Stop him!"

"He's gettin' away!"

"Tracey's got

my hairbrush!"

The chase began again.

The robber ran

into a supermarket

and out of it,

up an escalator

and down,

down an escalator

and up.

Into a lift,

and up and down

and up and down

and out.

Into a pizza parlour and –

Mmm – out, with a stolen pizza

(deep pan – family size – extra pepperoni).

The robber was little.

The robber was quick.

He twisted and turned

and ducked and weaved

and *nearly* got away.

The children couldn't catch him.

The police couldn't catch him.

Mrs Gaskitt couldn't catch him.

The robber ran out into the car park.

"I'll steal a car," he thought.

"I'll get away. Mmm – this pizza's good."

Suddenly, there was *Mr Gaskitt.*

"Out of my way," growled the robber.

"No," said Mr Gaskitt.

"I may be little," growled the robber, "but I'm hard."

The robber tried to run round Mr Gaskitt, but Mr Gaskitt was too wide for him.

He tried to punch Mr Gaskitt, but Mr Gaskitt didn't feel a thing.

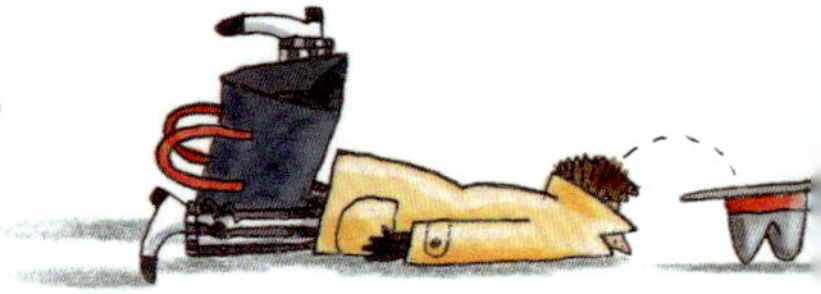

He tripped over his own enormous bag and fell down flat.

Mr Gaskitt *sat on him*.

Chapter Nine
What Horace Saw

Moments later, when the police

and the children

and the Christmas shoppers

and Mrs Gaskitt

and Gus and Gloria

and the TV reporter

(with her camera man and sound engineer)

arrived, all hot and out of breath,

there was the flat and captured robber,

and there was Mr Gaskitt,

cool and calm and eating pizza.

Then the police grabbed the robber.

Mrs Gaskitt hugged Gus and Gloria.

Mr Gaskitt hugged Mrs Gaskitt.

And Gus and Gloria hugged him.

Meanwhile, at his friend's house,

live on TV,

Horace saw it all!

"I know them!" he cried.

"No, you don't," said his friend.

"Yes, I do – they live in my house."

"No, they don't."

"Yes, they do – it's Mr and Mrs

and Gus and Gloria."

Horace purred with pride.

"I'm their cat."

Back at the car park

the police and the TV reporter

were asking questions,

and Gus and Gloria, mostly,

were answering them.

"He's our dad!"

"She's our mum!"

Mr Blotter was marching

the other children back to the bus.

The robber was on his way to jail.

There was talk of a reward.

Suddenly, Mr Gaskitt looked at his watch.

"Oh no!" he cried.

"Is that the time – I've got to go."

Mr Gaskitt kissed his wife and children –

"Goodbye, darlings!"

"Bye-bye, Dad!"

– and hurried off.

Chapter Ten

Mr Gaskitt Goes to Work

Mr Gaskitt was driving along.

"Soon be there now," he said to himself.

He switched on the radio –

"ROBBER GETS CLEAN AWAY, POLICE BAFFLED!" – and switched it off again.

"I really *must* get that radio fixed," thought Mr Gaskitt.

Mr Gaskitt turned left, drove past an automatic barrier,

and into a car park.

He squeezed out of his car and hurried into a lift.

Up went Mr Gaskitt: first floor, second floor, third floor … fourth floor.

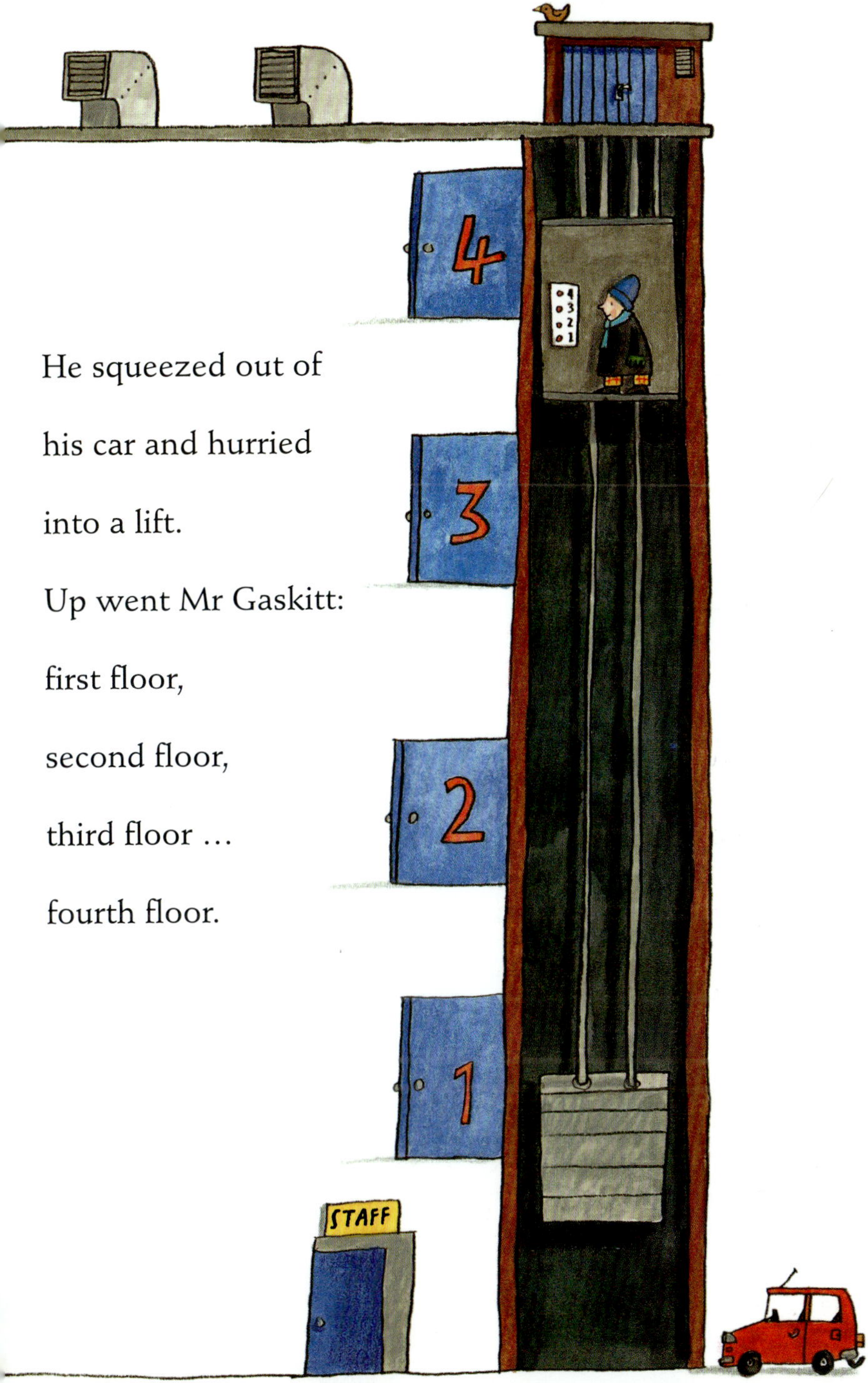

Mr Gaskitt entered a small room.

He grabbed the kettle

and made a quick cup of tea.

He looked at his watch.

"What a rush!" he thought.

Mr Gaskitt got ready.

He put on his red

working trousers

and his red

working coat,

his red working

hat and gloves,

his black

working boots

and his white

working whiskers.

"Ho, ho, ho!"

cried Mr Gaskitt,

and he went

to work.

Chapter Eleven

Mr Gaskitt Comes Home

Mr Gaskitt sat in his grotto

with children on his lap all day long.

He was the perfect Santa:

kind and *comfy*, like a big soft bed.

At half past five

Mr Gaskitt came home.

He took off his plastic mac,

his overcoat,

his anorak,

his jacket,

his three scarves

and his two pairs of gloves.

“Cup of tea, Dad,” said Gloria.

He took off four jumpers

and a tie,

two shirts

and a pair of trousers.

"Evening paper, Dad," Gus said.

Mr Gaskitt sat in his chair.

He drank his tea and

read the paper.

"FATHER CHRISTMAS

SAVES THE DAY!"

said the headlines.

That evening the Gaskitts –

all four of them *and* Horace –

watched a sad old movie on TV.

They shared the popcorn,

wiped their eyes and waited ...

for the happy ending.

Kitty
You are now leaving a Gaskitts book
Bye-bye!